The Light Within

The Light Within

A book for quiet thought and healing

Paintings by Kenneth Evans
Poems by Ann Ford

KEN EVANS PRINTS

© Ann Evans 1990
Published in Great Britain
by Ken Evans Prints,
Eggmoor Lane Cottage,
Chardstock, Devon.

ISBN 0 9512961 0 8

Printed in Somerset by Wincanton Litho

Cover by K. A. Evans
Designed by A. C. Ford

Contents

Introduction

For those who feel they are powerless to do much that is constructive towards righting the wrongs that they see in the world, this book may be a practical answer.

We can all become involved in the deepest spiritual healing of the world's ills. This is very real, perhaps even more real than actions. It can be done anywhere: at home, in the garden, at work, waiting for the bus, sitting on the train ... even if only for a few minutes.

To be quiet within oneself and to tune in to the spiritual dimension can be learnt. Set aside time for it. Be quiet, relax, forget personal anxieties, breathe deeply and allow the material world to pass by for a while.

Give yourself up to God so that God's powers can be given out through you to wherever they are needed at that moment anywhere in the world – or even the universe.

Allow yourself to be a channel for good, for peace. for love, for light and for healing. You will then be an active spiritual healer in the world, uplifting it, transforming it and filling it with the good the Creator intends it to be filled with.

1

Welcome
to the world of the spirit,
to the world of light,
to the world of reality
and clear-sightedness.

You will see with new eyes,
hear with new ears,
know what you have known
for a long time:

I AM HERE
always.

Come,
there is much for you to see
and to learn
and to do.

2

The work
I entrust to you
is to surrender yourself
completely
to My love
at every moment
in your life.

To the extent
that you are surrendered,
will I be able
to love and work
in the world.

You will not know
while you are on the earth
what effect
your surrender
is having in the world,
but remember:
it is My work
and it is all important
to Me.

It is very simple
for you:
surrender
absolutely!

3

Breathe in My strength,
fill your lungs with Me;
breathe in My love,
fill your heart with fire;
breathe in My wisdom,
let your mind be open;
breathe in My life,
let it flow through your veins.

Breathe out to the world
all the goodness of Me;
breathe out to the weak
My strength and My health;
breathe out on My children
My love and My laughter;
breathe out on My earth
My life and My all.

4

I found myself outside the world
and then, yet further still;
outside the universe I was,
beyond my mind and will.

Out there, so many miles away,
the light was gold yet dim;
the life of everything was there,
I, too, filled to the brim.

I felt a great relief to be
quite outside everything,
it made the worries we all have
seem petty, silly, nothing.

I saw how suns and moons are filled
with yellow, goodly light,
how all our cares and all of us
are seen from that great height.

I knew the greatness of the One
who made it all, and cares
what happens to the smallest thing
although still unawares.

The presence of the Mighty One
is ever up above,
the presence of the Giving One
fills everything with love.

5

Breathe in ME,
breathe out ME:

This is your work,
your work with Me;

Important work,
work of the spirit;

Work of love,
why you are here.

6

Breathe in My strength,
breathe in My power;

Breathe in My life,
breathe in My fullness;

Breathe in My awareness,
breathe in My love.

Breathe out over My world,
breathe out to My universe;

Breathe out in My heavens,
breathe out to Me.

Breathe out My greatness,
breathe out My wisdom;

Breathe out My infinity,
breathe out My all.

7

In tune
with the earth,

in time
with My breath,

in harmony
with Me.

8

Breathe in My light,
breathe in My soul,
breathe in the world
        and hold it there.

While it rests in your heart,
pulsating and pure,
stay still and wait
        with no fear.

Breathe on it, love,
breathe on it, life,
breathe on it, light,
        it is My soul.

Then
let it go.

9

Fill your body with Me,
fill every limb with Me;
see My light, see My life
re-charging your bones.

Breathe in from the earth,
breathe in through your feet;
breathe in strength and good,
breathe in from Me.

Breathe out from your head,
breathe out from your heart;
breathe out from your hands,
breathe out through your skin:

To the trees, to the plants,
to all creatures, to the earth,
to the planets, to the universe,
breathe out all – of ME.

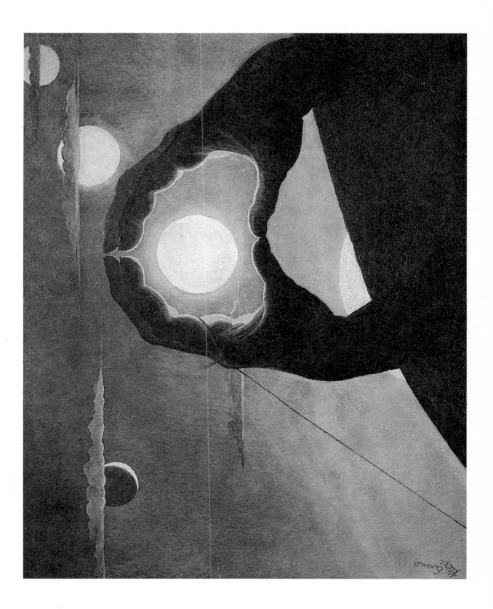

10

Breathe for My world;
breathe in My air,
breathe in My life,
breathe in ME.

Breathe out yourself,
breathe out My love,
breathe out My joy,
breathe out ME.

Breathe with ease,
breathe with laughter,
breathe with lightness,
breathe ME.

11

How slowly we walk
in the path of wisdom,
fumbling on our way;

How quietly You lead
on the path of life,
prodding us gently each day.

12

I saw a figure
like a tree,
floating above the clouds ...
free.

Her arms were branches,
full in leaf,
fluttering in the breeze ...
free.

Her body, the tree,
hair streaming out,
flowing above her head ...
free.

Who can she be,
quiet in face,
looking right into me?
silently.

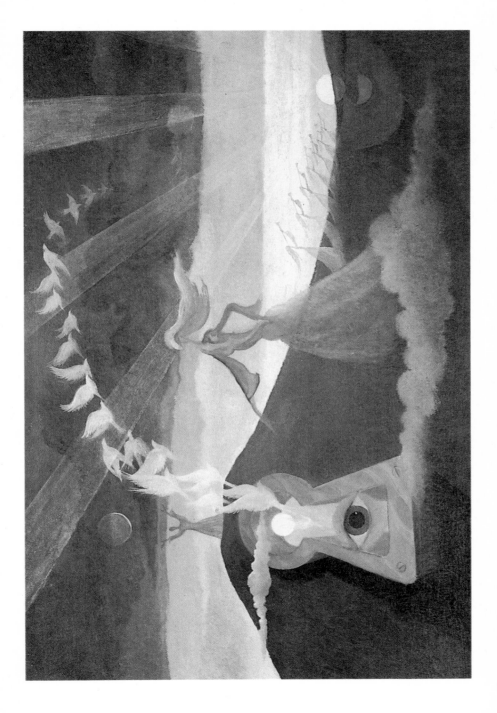

13

We are all on the road
drawn towards You,
yet each of us travels *with* You.

Let's hold hands, be glad
that YOU ARE HERE!
and *we* are on Your path.

Words do not matter —
rather use none —
You *are* the words and the song.

You are all thoughts
afire with love:
we, now, must learn to be flame.

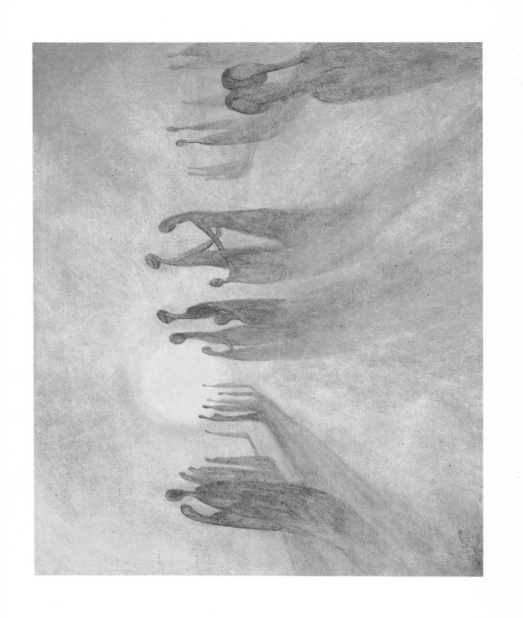

14

When the sun
shines through the mist,
we can see;

When the sun
shines through the mist,
we can know.

When Your light
shines through our mists,
we can be;

When Your light
shines through our mists,
we can sow ...

Your seeds
forever.

15

Breathe on My world,
breathe from your heart;

Breathe out My life,
breathe from My heart.

My life is yours,
My heart in you;

Breathe out to all
in all you do.

Notes about the Authors

For over twenty years, Kenneth Evans and Ann Ford, unknown to one another - Kenneth as an artist and Ann as a nun - found themselves being drawn closer and closer to the spiritual in the world.

Kenneth knew himself to have healing gifts and he concentrated on listening to creative forces in nature, portraying what he understood and saw in painting.

Ann, as a nun, concentrated on distant healing by praying for individuals and the world and also working as a nurse in Africa.

When Kenneth and Ann met in 1976, they realised that the same forces had now brought them together for a purpose: to express, both in paintings and in words, the *fact* of the spiritual and its tremendous power for good in the world.

They married and had two daughters, Jessie and Charlotte. Kenneth continued to paint every day and Ann to write poetry. They also worked together as healers.

Then, in 1987, quite suddenly, Kenneth died. Ann now continues to write and to heal. She lives in Devon with her daughters.